D1061017

WITHDRAWN

SIMPLE
MACHINE
PROJECTS

Making Machines with Springs

Chris Oxlade

heinemann
raintree

Edited by James Benefield and Erika Shores
Designed by Steve Mead
Original illustrations © Capstone Global Library Ltd
Picture research by Jo Miller
Production by Victoria Fitzgerald
Originated by Capstone Global Library Ltd
Printed and bound in China by Leo Paper Group

18 17 16 15 14
10 9 8 7 6 5 4 3 2 1

Library of Congress Cataloging-in-Publication Data
Oxlade, Chris, author.
  Making machines with springs / Chris Oxlade.
     pages cm.—(Simple machine projects)
Includes bibliographical references and index.
  ISBN 978-1-4109-6803-6 (hb)—ISBN 978-1-4109-6810-4
(pb)—ISBN 978-1-4109-6824-1 (ebook) 1. Springs (Mech-
anism)—Juvenile literature. 2. Simple machines—Juvenile
literature. I. Title.

TJ210.O95 2015
621.8′24—dc23   2014013823

**This book has been officially leveled by using the F&P Text
Level Gradient™ Leveling System.**

Acknowledgments
We would like to thank the following for permission to
reproduce photographs: All photos Capstone Studio: Karon
Dubke except: Alamy: cala image, 5, Richard McDowell, 27;
Chris Oxlade, 26; Dreamstime: Stanko07, 14; Getty Images:
Image Source/Photodisc, 4; iStockphotos: John Bradley, 7,
tungphoto, 29 (top); Shutterstock: Arve Bettum, 13, chen
peng, 29 (bottom), Gavran333, 15, Pavel L Photo and Video,
20, 21, Pressmaster, 12.

Design Elements: Shutterstock: Timo Kohlbacher.

We would like to thank Harold Pratt and Richard Taylor for
their invaluable help in the preparation of this book.

Every effort has been made to contact copyright holders
of material reproduced in this book. Any omissions will
be rectified in subsequent printings if notice is given to
the publisher.

All the Internet addresses (URLs) given in this book were valid
at the time of going to press. However, due to the dynamic
nature of the Internet, some addresses may have changed, or
sites may have changed or ceased to exist since publication.
While the author and publisher regret any inconvenience this
may cause readers, no responsibility for any such changes can
be accepted by either the author or the publisher.

CONTENTS

Some words are shown in bold, **like this**. You can find out what they mean by looking in the glossary.

WHAT IS A SPRING?

Pressing a door handle, using the brakes on your bicycle, and stretching a rubber band are things you might do every day. Every time you do one of them, springs help you. For example, there is a spring inside a door handle that returns the handle to its normal position when you release it.

Springs are not simple machines (see the box on page 5), but people sometimes talk about them in the same way. Springs are found in many objects and things we use, and they can make certain jobs in our lives easier.

Have you ever used a pogo stick? The springs help you to bounce up and down.

You can stretch, squeeze, or bend a spring, but when you let go, it returns to its original shape. In this book, you'll see many examples of springs, and the projects will help you to understand how springs work.

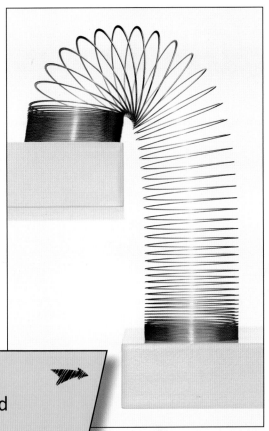

A Slinky spring is a very long **coil spring** that stretches and bends very easily.

SIMPLE MACHINES

Simple machines make our lives easier by helping us to do jobs such as lifting heavy loads, gripping objects tightly, and cutting tough materials. There are five simple machines. They are the **lever**, the **pulley**, the **wheel and axle**, the **ramp** (and the **wedge**), and the **screw**. Springs are not simple machines, but they often work with simple machines and do very useful jobs, too.

HOW SPRINGS WORK

You need the right materials for springs to work properly. Most springs are made of metal, but some are made from plastic. Rubber bands also work like springs. You can change the shape of these materials using **forces** (pushes and pulls), but they go back into their original shape afterward.

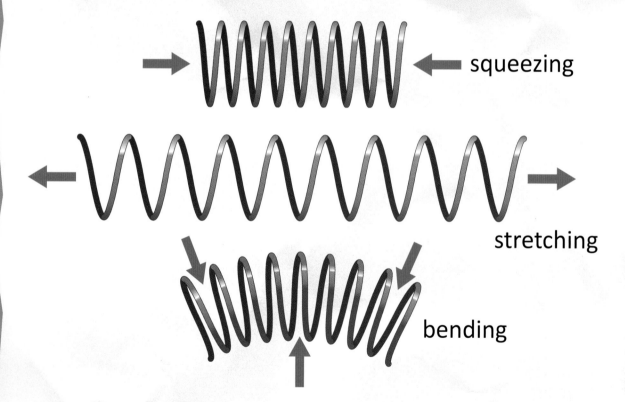

squeezing

stretching

bending

 You need two or more forces to make a spring change shape.

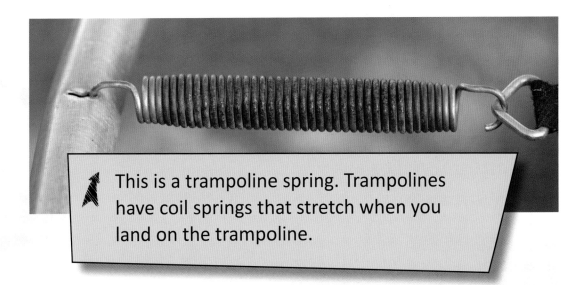

This is a trampoline spring. Trampolines have coil springs that stretch when you land on the trampoline.

Spring types

Springs come in many shapes and sizes, from tiny, delicate springs in watches to giant **suspension springs** on trucks. The most common kind of spring is the coil spring, which is made from a coil of wire. Some springs are designed to be stretched. Some are designed to be squeezed. Others are designed to be bent or twisted.

CHOOSING MATERIALS

We can only make springs from some materials. You couldn't make a spring out of modeling clay, because it wouldn't go back into its shape. And you couldn't make a spring from rock, because rock is **brittle**.

Squeezing, Stretching, and Bending Springs

In this project, you can see what forces you need to stretch, squeeze, and bend springs. You can also feel the pushes and pulls springs make, and how springs go back into shape.

What you need:
- the spring from a retractable ballpoint pen (ask an adult if you can take this from the pen)
- the spring from a clothespin (ask an adult to remove this from the clothespin)
- some rubber bands (in different sizes)
- a plastic ruler

1 Take the spring from a retractable ballpoint pen. Hold the two ends in your fingers (see picture). Pull gently to stretch the spring. Feel the pull that the spring makes on your fingers.

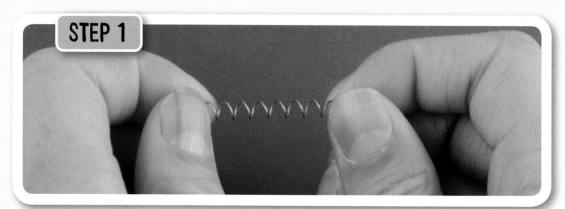

STEP 1

2 Try pushing the ends of the spring together instead. Feel the push that the spring makes on your fingers.

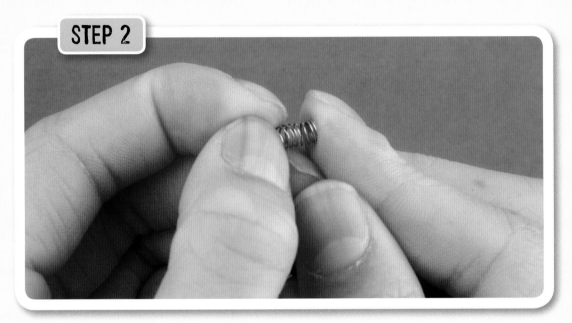

STEP 2

3 Now try bending the spring (see picture). Hold the ends in your fingers and turn the ends down to bend the spring over. What force can you feel now?

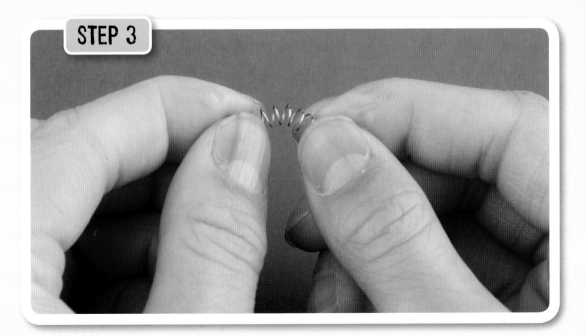

STEP 3

4 Push the two wire ends of the pin's spring together (see picture). Watch what happens to the spring. It twists instead of changing length or bending.

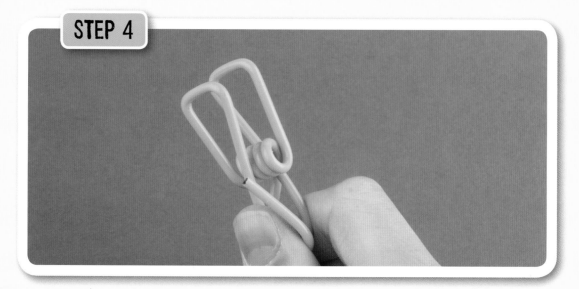

STEP 4

5 Choose a thin rubber band and try stretching it (see picture). Feel the pull it makes on your hands. Try stretching a thicker rubber band of the same length to see if the forces feel any different.

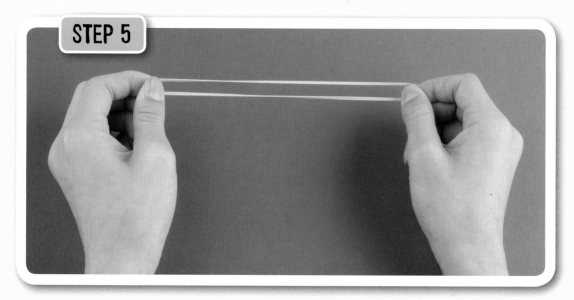

STEP 5

6 Put the plastic ruler over the edge of the table (see picture). Bend the ruler down by an inch or so and release it to see how a ruler works like a spring. Don't bend the ruler too far, or it will snap.

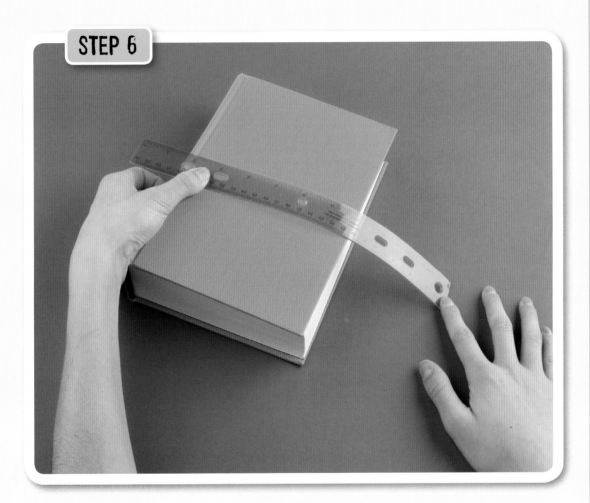

STEP 6

What did you find out?
As you stretch, squeeze, or bend a spring, the push or pull you need to make increases, and the more the spring pushes or pulls on you.

SPRING JOBS

Many simple gadgets have springs that help make them work. We've seen some examples already. For example, a pen needs a spring that squeezes (page 8), and a trampoline needs springs that stretch (page 7).

Springs for pushing back

Many springs do the job of returning part of a gadget into position after it has been moved. Think about video game controllers. The buttons and sticks of controllers have springs that push the buttons up.

A spring under each key on a keyboard pushes it back up after it is pressed.

Springs for pushing together

Some springs push the parts of gadgets together. For example, the springs inside battery compartments of electronic gadgets and toys keep batteries in place.

The springs inside a flashlight press the battery **terminals** against the bulb's contacts.

BUNGEE JUMPING

A bungee cord is like a very thick rubber band, and it works like a giant stretchy spring. As a bungee jumper falls, the bungee stretches, slowing down the jumper's fall.

SPRINGS IN HISTORY

Historians think that people started using springs about 3,500 years ago. At this time, people made tools, weapons, and ornaments from a metal called **bronze**. Historians have found jewelry with flat springs that held everything in place on clothing.

rope used as spring

You can see a rope spring on each side of this ballista.

Firing springs

Hundreds of years later, Greek and Roman armies fired heavy arrows with a machine called a ballista. This machine looked like a giant crossbow and was made out of wood. It had two powerful springs made from twisted ropes. This type of spring is called a torsion spring.

Clock springs

The first strong metal springs were made about 600 years ago. They were used in clocks. The spring was wound up with a key. As the spring unwound, it moved the parts of the clock.

The coiled strip of metal in this picture is the spring of a clock.

HOOKE'S SPRING

English scientist Robert Hooke was the first person who measured how springs work. In 1660, he realized that if you double the pull on a spring, it stretches twice as much.

A Spring Catapult

In this project, you can make a model catapult that is powered by a rubber band. The rubber band is twisted so that it creates a force that launches a piece of paper.

What you need:
- a small, strong cardboard box, 3 x 3 x 3 in. (8 x 8 x 8 cm)
- scissors
- 3 popsicle sticks
- sticky tape
- a medium-sized, medium-thick rubber band
- the cap from a screw-top bottle
- all-purpose glue

1 Stand the box on your work surface, with the 3-inch-wide edge facing upward (see picture below).

STEP 1

2 Ask an adult to help. With the tip of the scissors, pierce a horizontal hole half an inch (1 cm) long, 1 inch (2 cm) down, on opposite sides of the box.

STEP 2

3 Push a popsicle stick a short way into each hole (see how this is done in the picture, right). Push the sticks against the sides of the box and tape them in place.

STEP 3

4 Put a rubber band around the two sticks, about 1½ in. (4 cm) above the box. Put another stick through the rubber band (see picture, right).

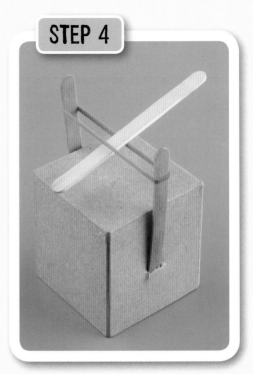

5 Wind the popsicle stick around and around until the rubber band is tightly wound. Release the stick. One end should press against the box.

6 Glue a bottle top to the top end of the stick (see picture below).

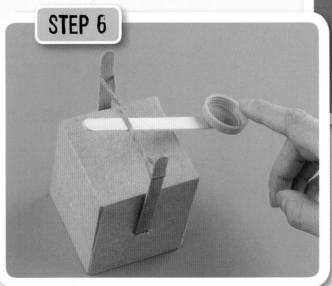

7 Scrunch up a small piece of paper and put it into the cap (see below). Pull the cap down and then let go.

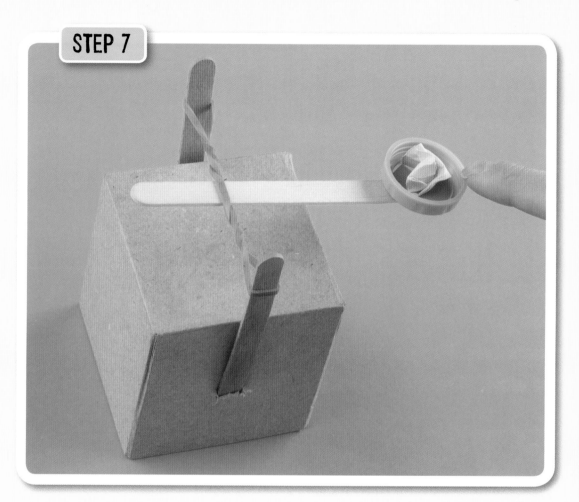

STEP 7

What did you find out?
The twisted rubber band works like a spring. Because it is twisted, it makes a push on the popsicle stick, trying to make it spin. This push launches the paper.

STORING ENERGY WITH SPRINGS

In some gadgets, we use springs to store energy so that the energy can be used later.

There is a spiral-shaped spring inside a wind-up toy (also called a **clockwork** toy). When you wind the toy, the spring gets tighter. This stores the energy you used to do the winding. When you let go of the toy, the spring unwinds. The spring moves the parts of the toy, making it work. The toy moves until the spring is unwound.

If you wind up this toy robot, it will move along a surface until the spring inside is unwound.

Rubber bands can store energy in the same way as springs. A wind-up model plane has a rubber band. As you wind the propeller, the band twists, storing energy. When you release the propeller, the band unwinds, slowly releasing the energy to turn the propeller.

The energy in the twisted rubber band can keep the propeller moving for more than a minute.

CLOCKWORK FROM CLOCKS

Wind-up toys are also called clockwork toys because the springs that store energy in them were first used to power clocks. Until about 100 years ago, most moving toys were wind-up toys.

Rubber Band Power

Here's a project that shows how a rubber band can store the energy needed to push along a simple vehicle.

1 Get the cardboard tube. Measure 4 inches from one end and make marks around the tube. Join the marks to make a line around the tube.

What you need:
- a cardboard tube (such as a paper towel roll)
- scissors
- 2 old CDs or DVDs (check with an adult that you are allowed to use them)
- all-purpose glue
- a popsicle stick
- a long pencil
- a large rubber band, about 4 inches (10 cm) long
- sticky tape

STEP 1

2 Cut carefully around the tube along the line.

3 Glue around the edge of the cardboard at one end of the tube. Stand the glued end of the tube in the center of one of the CDs.

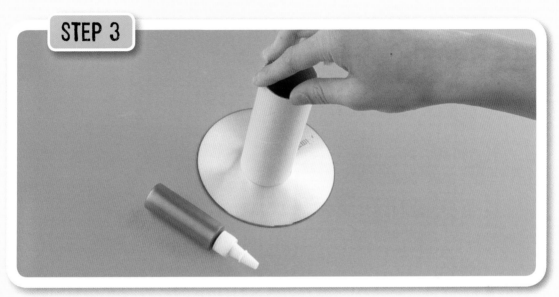

STEP 3

4 Glue the other end of the tube, turn the tube over, and stand it in the center of another CD (see picture below). Allow the glue to dry.

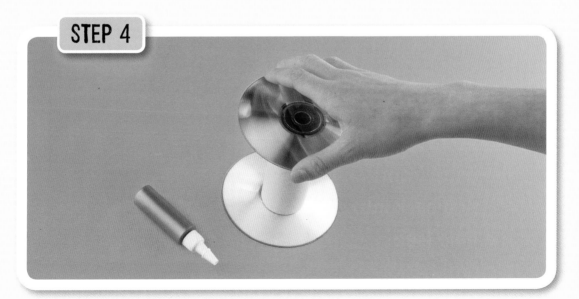

STEP 4

5 Break a popsicle stick in half. Put one half through one end of the rubber band. With a pencil, push the other end of the band through the hole in one of the CDs and out of the other end of the tube.

STEP 5

6 Hold onto the end of the band where it comes out of the other CD. Put the pencil through the band and put it across the CD to stop the band from slipping back into the hole (see picture).

STEP 6

7 Tape the popsicle stick to the CD to stop the stick from spinning.

STEP 7

8 Wind the pencil around the CD 15 to 20 times. Don't wind the band too many times, or the pencil will be too tight against the CD.

STEP 9

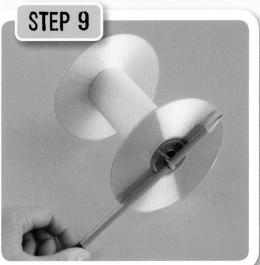

9 Let the pencil go. The toy should move. The pencil shouldn't stop it from moving, but if it does, try a shorter pencil.

What did you find out?

When you wind the pencil, you twist the rubber band. This stores energy in the rubber band. When you remove the pencil, the band unwinds again, pushing the vehicle along the worktop.

SPRINGS IN COMPLEX MACHINES

Many complicated machines contain springs. The springs do all the jobs we have seen so far in this book. They keep parts of the machines in position, they press parts of machines together, they absorb bumps, and they store energy.

Bicycle springs

There are springs on all bicycles. The photo (right) shows you where they are—near the brakes. When you let go of a brake lever on the handlebars, springs pull the rubber brake pads away from the wheels.

Bicycle brake springs keep the brakes off when you don't need them.

Cars, trucks, and buses have large suspension springs. These springs let the vehicle's wheels go up and down as they go over bumps in the road. This makes riding in these vehicles more comfortable.

The suspension spring on a race car must be very strong to support the weight.

RUBBER SPRINGS

Some trucks and trains have rubber springs instead of metal springs. The rubber springs are big blocks of rubber, sometimes with air inside. These springs are squeezed when the truck or train goes over a bump.

FACTS AND FUN

AMAZING SPRINGS

In 1933, a Japanese carmaker built a car with a huge clockwork spring inside. The car could drive up to 43 miles (70 kilometers) before it needed to be wound up again.

In 2006, a man bungee jumped from the Macau Tower in China. He fell 653 feet (199 meters) before the bungee cord stopped him—just 112 feet (34 meters) from the ground!

The most expensive bed mattresses contain more than 2,000 coiled springs to keep sleepers comfortable at night.

Some para-athletes who have lost legs run in sprint races wearing high-tech springs called blades.

A Roman ballista (spring-powered crossbow) could fire an arrow weighing about 55 pounds (25 kilograms) more than half a mile (1 kilometer).

SPRINGS TODAY

Simple machines, such as levers and wedges, were invented thousands of years ago. So was the spring. It didn't look like the metal springs we have today. Instead, early springs were made of twisted plant fibers. Today, springs are more important than ever, because they are an important part of many complex machines. Springs will certainly be useful for thousands of years to come.

What and where are these springs?

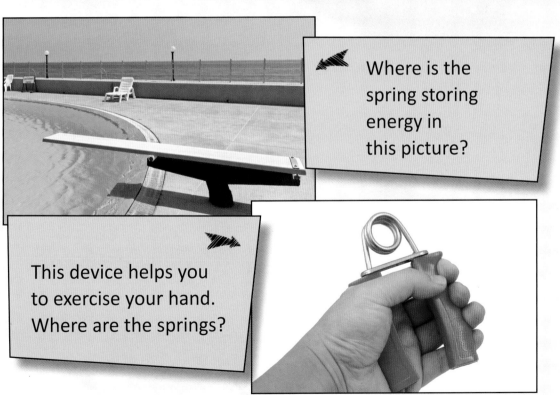

Where is the spring storing energy in this picture?

This device helps you to exercise your hand. Where are the springs?

GLOSSARY

brittle material that snaps easily. Chocolate is brittle.

bronze type of metal, made by mixing copper and tin

clockwork mechanism that is worked by the energy stored in a coiled spring

coil spring spring that is made of a piece of wire twisted into a spiral shape

force push or a pull

lever long bar that is pushed or pulled against a fulcrum to help move heavy loads or cut material

pulley simple machine made up of wheels and rope, used to lift or pull objects

ramp simple machine used to lift heavy objects

screw simple machine that has a spiral-shaped thread, used to attach or lift materials

suspension spring spring allowing vehicle wheels to move up and down as vehicles go over bumps

terminals metal contacts on a battery where electricity flows in and out of the battery

wedge simple machine used to split apart materials

wheel and axle simple machine made up of a wheel on an axle, used to turn or lift objects

FIND OUT MORE

Books

Deane-Pratt, Ade. *Simple Machines* (How Things Work).
   New York: PowerKids, 2012.

Hewitt, Sally. *Springs* (Science Starters). North Mankato, Minn.:
   Stargazer, 2005.

McGregor, Harriet. *Magnets and Springs* (Sherlock Bones Looks
   at Physical Science). New York: Windmill, 2011.

Web sites

Facthound offers a safe, fun way to find
Internet sites related to this book. All
of the sites on Facthound have been
researched by our staff.

Here's all you do:
Visit *www.facthound.com*
Type in this code: 9781410968036

INDEX